DISASTERS AT SEA

MICHAEL WOODS AND MARY B. WOODS

LERNER PUBLICATIONS COMPANY
MINNEAPOLIS

東區一號
DONG QU YI HAO

To Margaret E. Woods

Editor's note: Determining the exact death toll following disasters is often difficult—if not impossible—especially in the case of disasters that took place long ago. The authors and the editors in this series have used their best judgment in determining which figures to include.

Lerner Publications Company
A division of Lerner Publishing Group, Inc.
241 First Avenue North
Minneapolis, MN 55401 U.S.A.

Website address: www.lernerbooks.com

Library of Congress Cataloging-in-Publication Data

Woods, Michael, 1946–
    Disasters at sea / by Michael Woods and Mary B. Woods.
      p. cm. — (Disasters up close)
    Includes bibliographical references and index.
    ISBN 978–0–8225–6773–8 (lib. bdg. : alk. paper)
    1. Shipwrecks—Juvenile literature. 2. Marine accidents—Juvenile literature.
  I. Woods, Mary B. (Mary Boyle), 1946– II. Title.
  G525.W899 2008
  910.4'52—dc22   2006036729

Manufactured in the United States of America
1 2 3 4 5 6 – DP – 13 12 11 10 09 08

Contents

Introduction

THE *AL-SALAM BOCCACCIO 98* WAS A FERRYBOAT. IT CARRIED CARS AND PEOPLE ACROSS THE RED SEA. THAT NARROW BODY OF WATER IS BETWEEN EGYPT AND SAUDI ARABIA IN THE MIDDLE EAST. ABOUT FOURTEEN HUNDRED PEOPLE WERE ON THE *AL-SALAM* ON FEBRUARY 2, 2006. MANY WERE WORKERS GOING HOME TO EGYPT FROM THEIR JOBS IN SAUDI ARABIA.

About two hours after the ship left Saudi Arabia, a fire broke out. Thick black smoke poured out from below the *Al-Salam*'s deck, or floor. "There was a blaze down below," said passenger Nadir Jalal Abd al-Shafi. "The crew said, 'Don't worry, we will put it out.'"

The crew tried to put out the fire. They used hoses to spray water on the fire. However, the fire spread. The crew sprayed more and more water on it. That water collected inside the *Al-Salam*. Slowly, the water flooded the ship.

Passengers begged the crew and the captain to turn the ship around. It was still 56 miles (90 kilometers) from Egypt's port of Safaga. The passengers believed they could get back to Saudi Arabia safely. However, the captain decided to continue toward Egypt. The *Al-Salam* kept sailing and flooding. "If we had only gone back to Saudi Arabia," said passenger Abdul Rahman.

"We stayed cruising six hours at sea," said passenger Nazih Zaki, "and then the boat started to tip. The ship is five stories tall, but it took less than 15 minutes for it to go down."

As the ship sank, passengers jumped into the Red Sea. The water was 2,600

A survivor *(center)* of the sinking of the *Al-Salam Boccaccio 98* ferry receives help from rescue workers on February 4, 2006.

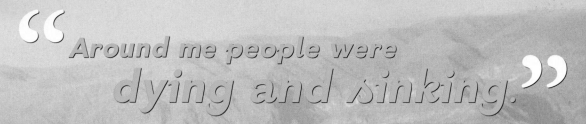

The *Al-Salam* in 1999. The ferryboat sank in the Red Sea in 2006 with fourteen hundred passengers on board.

feet (792 meters) deep. The ship didn't carry enough life preservers for all fourteen hundred passengers. These jackets keep people floating until help arrives. Many of the passengers could not swim. They drowned in the sea. Survivors crowded into the few available lifeboats. Because the lifeboats were overloaded with people, some of the boats sank and more people lost their lives.

Ahmed Elew swam for several hours and saw one overloaded lifeboat sink. "Around me people were dying and sinking," he said.

The *Al-Salam* sank around one o'clock in the morning. It was pitch dark. Winds blowing at 65 miles (105 km) per hour made big waves. "The weather was terrible," said Salah Jomaa. He was the captain of another boat on the Red Sea. "It was so bad, you couldn't imagine."

Survivors had to fight for their lives in that rough, cold water all night until rescue boats arrived. Some survivors were in the water for fourteen hours. Dead bodies also were floating in the water. More than one thousand people died in this disaster at sea.

What Are Disasters at Sea?

DISASTERS ARE EVENTS THAT HARM A LARGE NUMBER OF PEOPLE. THIS BOOK IS ABOUT DISASTERS THAT HAPPEN TO PEOPLE ON BOATS AND SHIPS. BOATS AND SHIPS CAN CATCH FIRE, EXPLODE, SAIL INTO STORMS OR ROUGH SEAS, OR CRASH. THESE ACCIDENTS OR EVENTS CAN CAUSE VESSELS TO SINK.

People must abandon (get off) the ship or die. Even then the survivors may have terrible experiences. Life rafts filled with people floated all night in icy cold water after the ferryboat *Estonia* sank in the Baltic Sea in 1994.

"We sat and hugged each other [to keep warm] all the time," said Kent Harstedt, a survivor of the *Estonia* sinking. "Little by little [other survivors] died and were left lying in the raft. So we were sitting there among dead bodies in the raft." You'll read more about the *Estonia* later in this book.

BOAT OR SHIP?

Boats are small. Ships are large. Ships are big enough to carry their own boats, such as lifeboats. To tell the difference, remember this saying: "A boat can fit on a ship, but a ship can't fit on a boat."

SEA THAT WATER

Some of the disasters you will read about have happened at sea. You will also learn about disasters that have occurred on oceans, large saltwater lakes, smaller freshwater lakes, and rivers.

Most disasters on water involve boats or ships carrying a lot of people. It is terrible if one or two people die when their boat sinks. The families and friends of those people are very sad. However, is it a disaster? No. Disasters harm a lot of people. Some disasters on water kill or injure thousands of people.

This boat sank off the coast of Croatia in 2006.

SAFE SHIPS

Traveling in a cruise ship or ferry is very safe. In the United States, fewer than one hundred passengers die each year in boat or ship accidents. In contrast, about forty thousand people die each year in car accidents.

In other countries, traveling on the water may be more dangerous. Some countries have fewer safety rules than the United States. In addition, shipowners may not follow the rules.

Despite safety rules, even one disaster at sea can cause hundreds of deaths. In 2002, for instance, more than eighteen hundred people died in one disaster. It happened when a ship named the *Joola* sank off the coast of Africa.

WORSE SEA DISASTERS AHEAD?

Modern ships and boats are safer than ever before. Modern ships are built with steel. Steel is much stronger than wood, which used to be the material with which boats and ships were made. Modern ships have more safety equipment, such as fire extinguishers. The crews on these ships receive top-level safety training.

However, there may be worse disasters at sea in the future. That's because companies are building bigger and bigger cruise ships. People take vacations on these passenger ships. Some cruise ships can carry five thousand people. Just one accident on such a huge ship could be a terrible disaster at sea.

DID YOU KNOW?

Which do you think is more dangerous: sailing on a cruise ship *(below)* on the ocean or riding in a motorboat on a small lake? The motorboat is more dangerous. In the United States every year, about six hundred to eight hundred people die every year in recreational boating accidents. In many years, no passengers die in cruise ship disasters.

"We saw **bodies floating** by the hundreds, the hundreds, **the hundreds.**"

—Haidar el Ali, rescue team diver, for the Joola, 2002

The *Joola*, a ferryboat from Senegal, capsized on September 27, 2002, in the Atlantic Ocean.

April 27, 1865
THE SULTANA

This wood engraving shows the *Sultana* on fire and many of the soldiers who were on board in the water. Few people knew about the *Sultana* disaster because the newspapers were filled with stories about another tragedy. Those stories were about the killing of President Abraham Lincoln on April 14, 1865.

Thousands of Union soldiers were waiting for a ride home. They had gathered in Vicksburg, Mississippi, on April 24, 1865. Many of the soldiers had been away for four long years. They had fought in the American Civil War (1861–1865). That war between the North (the Union) and South (the Confederacy) had recently ended.

Soldiers cheered when their ride arrived. It was a wooden steamship named the *Sultana*. The ship would take the soldiers up the Mississippi River.

The *Sultana* was built to carry 376 passengers. However, the soldiers were very eager to get home. Hundreds more rushed on board. *"We boarded this boat 2,200 strong, all joyful and happy that peace had come at last, and anxious to get home to the loved ones once more,"* said Union soldier James Robert Collins. Including other passengers and the crew, about 2,300 people were on the *Sultana*.

Soldiers were sleeping on the *Sultana's* decks on the night of April 27, 1865. Without any warning, the *Sultana's* engines exploded. The explosion tore apart the ship. Hundreds of soldiers were thrown into the cold waters of the

Mississippi River. Others were trapped under heavy wooden boards that had been blown into the air and landed back on the deck.

The *Sultana*'s engines burned coal. That material looked like the charcoal in a barbecue grill. The explosion sprayed burning coal into the air. The red-hot coals fell onto the ship and many of the soldiers. *"The immense cloud of hot coals . . . rained down upon us and I could feel my flesh being burned and scorched as I lay there,"* said Collins.

The explosion and the hot coals set the *Sultana* on fire. *"Men were rushing [back and forth], trampling over each other in their endeavors to escape,"* said William H. Norton, a survivor of the disaster. Arthur A. Jones, another survivor, said, *"No tongue or writer's pen can describe it."*

Many of the soldiers could not swim. However, they jumped into the river rather than be burned to death. *"The river was full of men struggling with each other and grasping at every thing that offered [a] means of support,"* said Norton. *"As I arose to the surface, several men from the boat jumped upon me and we all went down together."*

One man who was in the river remembered the scene. *"[I] could see men jumping from all parts of the boat into the water, until it seemed black with men, their heads bobbing like corks, and then disappearing beneath the [water] never to appear again."*

About seventeen hundred people died in the *Sultana* disaster. Many of the survivors had scars from burns and other injuries. It was the worst civilian (nonmilitary) ship disaster in U.S. history.

> *"The immense cloud of hot coals . . . rained down upon us and I could feel my flesh being burned and scorched as I lay there.*
>
> —James Robert Collins, Sultana passenger, 1865

The *Sultana*, overloaded with Union soldiers heading home after the Civil War, is shown on the Mississippi River the day before the ship sank.

Recipe for Disaster

SHIPS AND BOATS ARE BUILT TO CARRY PASSENGERS. THEY ALSO CARRY CARGO (DIFFERENT KINDS OF GOODS). THEY MUST BE STRONG BUT LIGHT ENOUGH TO FLOAT.

To float, a ship must be watertight. It must have a hull that keeps out water. The sides, bottom, and deck of a ship make up its hull.

Water presses in on the sides and bottom of a ship. If the hull has a crack or hole, water will pour into the ship. Water can also press down onto a ship. During storms, huge waves may crash onto a ship's deck.

HOLES IN THE HULL

Most disasters at sea happen when something makes holes in a ship's hull. Water is heavy. A gallon (3.7 liters) of water weighs about 8 pounds (3.6 kilograms).

In only a short time, millions of gallons of water may pour through holes in a ship's hull. Ships have pumps to shoot water back out into the ocean. However, water may pour in faster than the pumps can pump it back out.

If too much water collects inside, it can make a ship too heavy to float. The ship will sink.

Everything on board the ships goes into the water. The ship's cargo sinks to the bottom of the ocean. Passengers and crew go into the water. If people can't keep their heads above water, they may drown. Without air, a person will die within four minutes.

Other people who go into the water in a disaster may freeze to death. Seawater often is very cold. Cold water takes heat away from the body. People may die from hypothermia. This condition occurs when the body gets too cold.

This cargo ship has a crack in its hull. The crack happened during a storm while the ship was at sea.

HOLES AREN'T THE ONLY PROBLEM

People also may die or get hurt while they are still on the ship. They may be injured by fires, explosions, crashes, bad weather, and human errors (mistakes).

Disasters at sea often have several causes. For example, the *Al-Salam Boccaccio 98* caught fire while sailing across the Red Sea. The captain could have turned back to shore. However, he decided to continue sailing. The ship sank in the middle of the Red Sea. A fire and a human error (the captain's bad decision) caused that disaster.

FEARSOME FIRES

Fire is one of the worst nightmares for people on a boat or ship. Fires can cause a disaster at sea in several ways. A fire may make a ship sink by burning holes in the hull so water pours in. Fires also may force people to leave the ship to avoid burning to death. When a building on land catches fire, people can escape by going outside. On the sea, however, people can escape the fire only by going into the water.

Going into the water may mean trading one danger for another. People in the water may drown. They may freeze to death. In some parts of the ocean, they may be attacked by sharks.

Fires on ships are especially dangerous for another reason. Ships have sealed windows to keep out the water. Passengers cannot open windows to let fresh air inside. Air-conditioning circulates air inside the ship. If there is a fire, the air-conditioning system may circulate smoke and poisonous gases from the fire. The gases can kill people or cause them to pass out so they cannot escape.

When a serious fire happens on a ship, passengers and crew have two terrible choices. One is to abandon ship and face the risks of being in the water. The other is to burn to death. As the fire destroys more and more of the ship, passengers may crowd to one end to escape. That is what happened on the *Sultana* in 1865. "The fire got so hot the men [started jumping] off the boat into the river," said Thomas Thorn, a passenger. "They kept dropping off until the water was black with them."

This Italian cruise ship, *Achille Lauro*, caught fire in the Indian Ocean in December 1994. Almost all the one thousand people on board escaped from the burning ship in lifeboats.

NAVIGATION ERRORS

The captain navigates, or steers, a ship. Electronic technology helps modern ships navigate safely. Radar (a device that uses radio waves to detect objects) keeps watch for dangers, such as other ships traveling in the same path on the water. Sonar (a device that uses sound waves to detect objects) scans for dangerous objects under the water. A Global Positioning System (GPS) tells the captain the ship's exact location. GPS is a network of satellites. These human-made objects in space circle Earth and send signals. Ships use signals from these satellites to stay on course.

The captain also steers clear of other ships or dangerous objects. Sometimes, however, captains make navigation errors. Ships can crash into objects, such as other ships or icebergs, the floating chunks of ice that have broken off glaciers. They can sail into water that is too shallow. If that happens, they can crash into rocks on the seafloor.

The ship might go off course and crash. Fog, mist, or heavy rain can make it more difficult to see clearly and navigate safely.

CRASHES

Crashes are another danger for ships. In the past, ships did not have radar, sonar, GPS, and other navigation aids. Ships relied on

WAR'S WORST DISASTERS

Wars have caused the world's worst disasters at sea. Three terrible disasters at sea happened near the end of World War II (1939–1945).

Submarines shot torpedoes at German passenger ships. Those ships carried wounded soldiers. They also carried people trying to escape the fighting in Europe.

More than seven thousand people died in January 1945 when a Soviet submarine torpedoed the *Wilhelm Gustloff (left)*. Just one month later, forty-five hundred people died on the *General von Steuben* when it was torpedoed by the Soviets. When the *Goya* sank after a torpedo attack by the Soviets in April that year, more than sixty-five hundred people died.

Ships use radar, sonar, and Global Positioning
Systems to navigate in the water.

crew members with binoculars to watch out for hazards. But even binoculars can't help people see through fog. When the lookouts could not see, the ship was in danger.

Crashes have caused many terrible disasters. The most famous disaster at sea happened when the passenger liner *Titanic* hit an iceberg in 1912. More than fifteen hundred people were killed. The world's worst peacetime disaster at sea happened in the Philippines in 1987, when the *Doña Paz* and an oil tanker called the *Vector* collided. More than four thousand people died in that disaster.

WAVES AND WINDS

High waves and fierce windstorms are another ingredient in the recipe for disasters at sea. Hurricanes and tropical storms can cause waves that may be 50 feet (15 m) high. Winds may howl at more than 60 miles (97 km) per hour.

Most modern seagoing ships are strong enough to sail safely through storms. Ships also use radar to spot storms far ahead. The captain can steer away from the storm and sail on a safe course.

In the past, however, bad weather caused many shipwrecks. Even in modern times, bad weather can threaten ships. Bad weather can also damage ships that are old and in poor condition.

BREAKING THE RULES

Ships can safely carry only a certain amount of weight. Too many passengers or too much cargo will overload a ship. An overloaded ship cannot sail safely. It may tip over.

Government agencies set rules about how much weight a ship can safely carry. Captains and crews, however, sometimes break the rules. To make more money for the shipowners, they allow too many passengers or too much cargo on board.

Breaking other rules also can turn a ship into a disaster waiting to happen. Ships may not carry enough lifeboats, for instance. They may not have enough life preservers. Crews may not have received proper safety training, so they don't know how to help others during an emergency.

> **"** *I struggled free and fell into the water. I couldn't hear anything anymore. There was just silence.* **The sea was on fire.** *My face was scalded. The water was very hot as if it were boiling water. I swam so fast. I don't know how I did it.* **"**
>
> —Arnel Galang, Doña Paz survivor, 1987

Relatives of victims of the *Doña Paz* disaster place a banner reading "This must never happen again" in front of coffins holding victims' remains. More than four thousand people died when the ship collided with an oil tanker in 1987.

April 14, 1912
THE *TITANIC*

This illustration shows the *Titanic* hitting an iceberg on its first voyage in 1912.

The *Titanic* was as famous in 1912 as the space shuttle is in modern times. The *Titanic* was the world's biggest and fanciest ship. On April 14, 1912, the *Titanic* was making its maiden (first) voyage across the Atlantic Ocean from Southampton, England, to New York Harbor. Some of the world's most famous and wealthiest people were on board. The ship was also carrying many emigrants (people who were leaving their home countries) on their way to new lives in the United States.

The *Titanic* carried 2,223 passengers and a crew of 899. Everyone felt quite safe. People said the *Titanic* was an unsinkable ship. It was built with technology that was new at that time. If water got into one part of the ship, doors would close and seal off the leak. The ship could safely continue its journey without sinking.

On the night of April 14, crew members spotted a huge iceberg. Icebergs are very dangerous to ships. Hitting an iceberg can break holes in a ship's hull. The *Titanic*, however, was going too fast to avoid hitting it. At 11:40 P.M., the *Titanic* crashed into the iceberg. *"I had just gone below [to my cabin] when the crash came,"* said Mrs. Peter Reniff, a passenger on board the ship. *"The shock was awful. Nearly all of the passengers thought that the Titanic could not sink. Some of them took the collision as a joke."*

Another passenger was twelve-year-old Ruth Becker. When the collision happened, Ruth rushed up to the main deck with her mother, brother, and sister. The crew were loading women and children into lifeboats. Ruth remembered, *"One [crew member] grabbed my sister, and another carried my brother into the lifeboat and yelled, 'All full!' My mother screamed. They let my mother on, but they left me behind."* Ruth got on the next lifeboat.

The *Titanic* did not have enough lifeboats for all the passengers. Women and children got off the ship first. Crew members had to threaten some male passengers with guns to make sure women and children could escape. *"Some of the passengers fought with such desperation to get into the lifeboats that the [guards] shot them, and their bodies fell into the ocean,"* said Dr. Washington Dodge, a passenger on the ship.

As the *Titanic* sank, many passengers who had not escaped in lifeboats jumped overboard. The water was only about 34°F (1°C). Young Ruth Becker described the scene she saw from her lifeboat: *"There fell upon the ear the most terrible noise that human beings ever listened to—the cries of hundreds of people struggling in the icy cold water, crying for help with a cry we knew could not be answered."* The lifeboats could not return to rescue more passengers for fear that the lifeboats would be overturned by those desperate to escape the frigid water.

The survivors in the lifeboats suffered for hours. They were wet and cold. By morning another ship, the *Carpathia*, arrived to rescue them. Ruth remembered what it was like on board the *Carpathia*: *"The women were hunting for their husbands, and when they could not find them, they knew they had gone down with the ship. It was an awful sight."* This disaster, one of the worst in history, killed 1,523 people.

The *Titanic* sets sail from Southampton, England, on April 10, 1912.

Disaster Ferries

MORE PEOPLE DIE EACH YEAR IN FERRYBOAT DISASTERS THAN IN DISASTERS INVOLVING ANY OTHER KIND OF VESSEL. FERRYBOATS, OR FERRIES, CARRY PEOPLE ACROSS BODIES OF WATER. FERRYBOATS MAY ALSO CARRY CARS AND TRUCKS. FERRYBOATS MAKE THEIR CROSSINGS ON REGULAR SCHEDULES. SOME FERRYBOATS MAKE SEVERAL TRIPS EACH DAY, SOMETIMES CARRYING HUNDREDS OF PASSENGERS ON EACH TRIP.

DANGER ZONES

Many ferryboat disasters happen in poor countries. People in many poor countries are more likely to travel by ferry because they don't have cars or other means of transportation. Sometimes too many passengers are allowed on board. So if an accident or disaster occurs, more people will be injured or killed.

Another problem occurs because often the governments of poor countries can't afford to pay

The British ferryboat *Herald of Free Enterprise* capsized off the coast of Belgium in the English Channel in 1987. A total of 193 people died.

TERRIBLE TYPHOON

A typhoon (a hurricane that occurs in the Pacific Ocean) that roared through the Sea of Japan in September 1954 caused a terrible disaster. The typhoon sank the passenger ship *Toya Maru*, killing 1,159 people. Four other ships sank in the same storm, raising the total death toll to 1,430.

safety inspectors. Safety inspectors enforce rules meant to keep passengers and crews safe. But if there are too few safety inspectors, the risk of a ferryboat being in poor condition or unsafe rises. The captains and crews of the boats often ignore the safety rules that do exist.

Some boat owners know they can get away with breaking the safety rules. Since ferryboats run on regular schedules, owners may require the boats to sail in stormy weather. They keep sailing to stay on schedule and make money— even if it risks people's lives.

DANGEROUS COUNTRY

One country, in particular, has a lot of disasters at sea. That country is the Philippines, an island nation in Southeast Asia made up of more than seven thousand islands.

People in the Philippines rely on ferryboats to travel from one island to another. The boats often are old and run-down. Since many Filipinos are poor, they have no choice except to travel on dangerous ferryboats.

In 2006 researchers from the British National Maritime Museum estimated that forty thousand people die each year in accidents in the waters of the Philippines. Most of those deaths are among ferryboat passengers.

Storage tanks at a chemical plant burn on the waterfront in Texas City, Texas, on April 16, 1947.

DISASTER AT SEA = DISASTER ON LAND

One disaster at sea was also a disaster for people on land. On April 16, 1947, a ship called the *Grandcamp* was anchored off Texas City, Texas. When the *Grandcamp* caught on fire, hundreds of curious people onshore gathered to watch. Suddenly, the ship exploded.

The blast tore apart people and buildings. The explosion set off more explosions and fires at chemical factories in Texas City. Hundreds of other buildings caught on fire. At least 581 people died in the disaster, and 5,000 were injured.

DISASTER ZONES

Shipwrecks can happen on oceans, seas, rivers, or lakes—anywhere that a ship or boat is carrying passengers. This map shows where the disasters described in this book have occurred. The boxed information describes where and when the disaster took place and the number of deaths that resulted.

WILHELM GUSTLOFF (South Baltic Sea) 1945 (7,000+ deaths)

ESTONIA (Baltic Sea) 1994 (852 deaths)

TOYA MARU (Sea of Japan) 1954 (1,159 deaths)

EUROPE

ASIA

GENERAL VON STEUBEN (South Baltic Sea) 1945 (4,500+ deaths)

GOYA (South Baltic Sea) 1945 (6,500+ deaths)

AFRICA

AL-SALAM BOCCACCIO 98 (Red Sea) 2006 (1,000+ deaths)

JOOLA (Atlantic Ocean) 2002 (1,800 deaths)

DOÑA PAZ (Philippines) 1987 (4,000+ deaths)

AUSTRALIA

ETHAN ALLEN
(Lake George) 2005
(20 deaths)

EMPRESS OF IRELAND
(Saint Lawrence River,
CAN) 1914
(1,012 deaths)

GENERAL SLOCUM
(East River) 1904
(1,200 deaths)

SULTANA
(Mississippi River)
1865 (1,700 deaths)

NORTH AMERICA

TITANIC
(North Atlantic Ocean)
1912 (1,523 deaths)

GRANDCAMP
(Texas City, TX)
1947 (581 deaths)

NEPTUNE
(Caribbean Sea)
1993 (1,700 deaths)

SOUTH AMERICA

September 28, 1994
THE *ESTONIA*

The *Estonia* is lifted from the bottom of the Baltic Sea in November 1994. The ferryboat sank September 28, 1994.

The *Estonia* was a huge ferryboat. It was built to carry people, cars, and trucks. The *Estonia*'s bow (front end) opened and closed, almost like a huge garage door. People could drive cars and trucks right into the *Estonia*.

After all the cars and people were on board, the Estonia's bow door closed. It had to stay tightly closed. If the door opened, water would pour into the ship.

On September 28, 1994, the *Estonia* loaded four hundred cars and trucks and 989 people in Tallinn, Estonia. The ship then started sailing across the Baltic Sea. It was a stormy night. Waves were more than 20 feet (6 m) high. That's higher than a two-story house. As the *Estonia* sailed, those waves eventually crashed through the bow door.

Around midnight, some of the passengers, who didn't know the bow door had broken, started hearing a strange noise. It sounded like metal clanging against metal. The noise got louder, and the *Estonia* began shaking.

"The noise woke me up," said passenger Einar Kukk, "and I could feel that the ship was listing [tilting to one side]. I ran up on deck."

Another passenger, Tom Johansson, left his cabin as the *Estonia* began to shake and tilt even more. "In the corridor, all around me, I saw people knocked down on the floor, with their heads beating against the doors and walls," he said. "Many were hurt so badly that they were unconscious."

Kukk and Johansson were lucky. A few minutes later, lights in the *Estonia* went off. Passengers who were still in their cabins could not find their way out. The ship tilted even farther onto its side. Walls became floors. Floors became ceilings.

"Women and children were running, shouting, falling over each other as on a skating rink," said passenger Carl Oevberg. "Nobody could stand up. The main dining room was a real bloodbath, with bodies flung all over the place when the ship capsized [turned upside down]."

Passenger Paul Barney managed to climb into a life raft. But his struggle to survive was just starting. The water in the Baltic Sea was ice cold. Huge waves crashed onto the life rafts. Other survivors floated in the water in life jackets.

The *Estonia* was a ferryboat that could carry hundreds of people and cars.

Survivors waited in the water for as many as six hours before help arrived. Some of them died. "We had people dying around us all the time of hypothermia," said Barney.

The clanging noise that people had heard just before the disaster was the sound of the *Estonia's* bow door breaking. When it opened, the *Estonia*

> " The main dining room was a *real bloodbath*, with bodies flung all over. . . . "
>
> —Carl Oevberg, Estonia passenger, 1994

was like a whale swimming through the water with its mouth open. Within minutes, the ship started to tip and sink. This disaster at sea killed 852 people.

Rescue, Relief, and Recovery

WHEN DISASTERS OCCUR ON LAND, THE VICTIMS USUALLY GET HELP QUICKLY FROM OTHER PEOPLE. IT MAY TAKE ONLY MINUTES FOR FIRE TRUCKS OR AMBULANCES TO ARRIVE. WHEN RESCUE WORKERS HAVE SPECIFIC STREET ADDRESSES, THEY KNOW EXACTLY WHERE TO GO TO PROVIDE HELP.

Disasters at sea are different from disasters on land. A ship may be in the middle of the ocean when disaster strikes. Help may be hundreds of miles away.

MINUTES COUNT

Getting help fast is very important when disasters at sea occur. People who go under the water may drown within four minutes. Passengers who are wearing life jackets or are sitting in lifeboats also need help fast. Some may have burns, bloody cuts, broken bones, or other injuries.

For others, cold water is the biggest danger. Water often is very cold. Cold water can cause people to freeze to death in only a few minutes.

PEOPLE HELPING PEOPLE

Efforts to rescue victims and save lives begin before a disaster at sea happens. These efforts start right on the ship. People on a ship often help save one another. Most crew members are properly trained to deal with emergencies. They are the ship's fire department, for instance, and its police department. Crew members are trained to help passengers when disaster strikes.

LIFESAVERS

The crew help passengers with lifesaving equipment. That equipment includes life jackets and lifeboats. Life jackets help people stay afloat in the water.

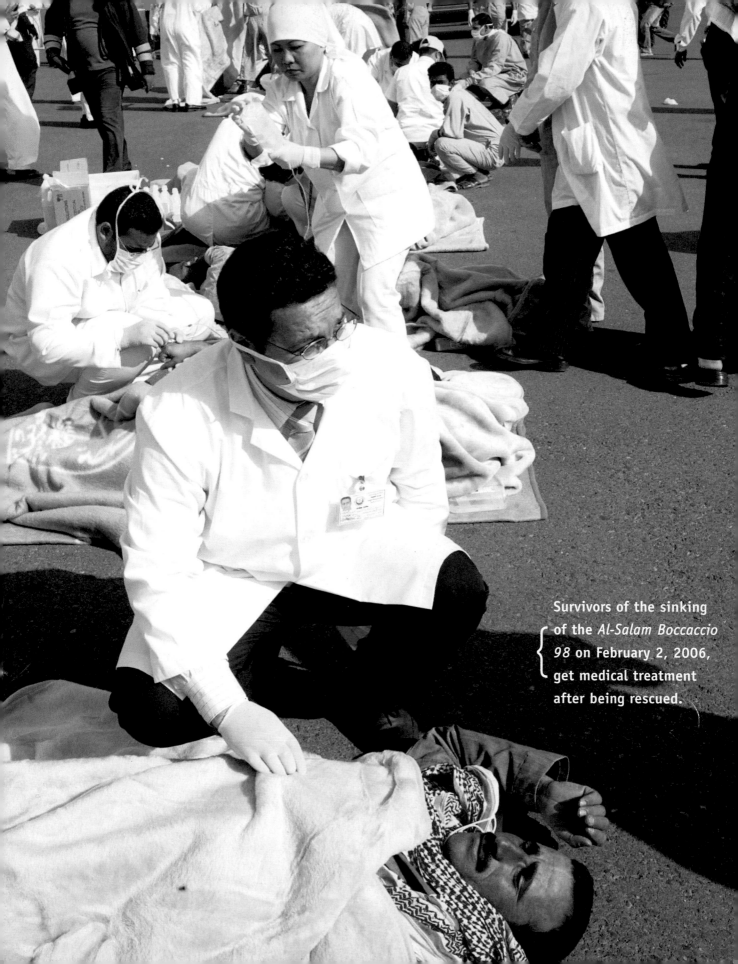

Survivors of the sinking of the *Al-Salam Boccaccio 98* on February 2, 2006, get medical treatment after being rescued.

Lifeboats allow victims to stay out of the water and keep warmer.

When passengers first board a ship, they receive safety lessons. Crew members teach passengers how to use life jackets. Passengers also learn how to quickly evacuate (get off) the ship in an emergency. These lessons are similar to the lessons flight attendants give at the beginning of every airplane flight.

If an evacuation is necessary, specially trained crew members help out. They make sure passengers have put on their life jackets correctly. They also load people into lifeboats.

NO ESCAPE

The *General Slocum* carried more than thirteen hundred people on the East River in New York City in 1904. When a fire broke out on the ship, passengers rushed for the life preservers. However, the life preservers were old. They had been poorly cared for. When passengers tried to use them, the life preservers fell apart. Then passengers rushed to the lifeboats. The boats were tied to the deck with strong wires. Nobody could cut the wires. Unable to use the lifeboats, about twelve hundred people were burned to death or jumped into the river and drowned.

AUTOMATIC SIGNALS

When a ship is in trouble, it broadcasts a distress signal that goes out to other ships. This call for help tells the location of the ship when the disaster struck. Nearby ships can hear the distress signal on their radios. These ships respond by sailing toward the disaster scene. The distress signal can also go to search-and-rescue centers onshore. Search-and-rescue teams are then sent to help.

One kind of device is the Emergency Position-Indicating Radio Beacon (EPIRB).

"SAVE OUR SHIP"

SOS was the first distress signal. People began using it in 1905. SOS is still the most famous call for help. The signal consists of sounds called dots and dashes sent out by radio in International Morse Code. Those dots and dashes form the letters *S-O-S*. People say that SOS means "Save Our Ship," "Survivors On Ship," "Save Our Sailors," "Stop Other Signals," or "Send Out Sailors."

" *I felt a terrific lurch. The floor [tilted]* ... *and* **water began pouring into the ship.** *In the dark,* **everyone was thrown together.** *Some were* **pushed over** *[the side into the ocean], some were* **stepped on.** *[People] were screaming and shouting in the dark.* **It was like hell on earth. "**

—*Kaichiki Yamakazi, Toya Maru survivor, 1954*

Guests on a cruise ship take part in mandatory safety lessons on their first day on the ship.

These electronic devices send out distress signals that go to a satellite that orbits Earth. The satellite sends distress signals to search-and-rescue airplanes and helicopters. The signal helps search-and-rescue aircraft to locate the ship. Lifeboats also have EPIRB devices. If the ship has sunk, search-and-rescue aircraft can locate survivors in lifeboats.

{ Emergency
Position-Indicating
Radio Beacon

Nearby ships often provide the first outside help for victims of a disaster. These ships pick up survivors. Once on board, the survivors get medical care, dry clothing, and hot food. The ship then takes the survivors to shore.

SEARCH AND RESCUE

Besides the lack of a specific address to provide to rescue teams, disasters on water are different from disasters on land in another way. When rescue workers arrive, they may find no disaster scene. The ship may have sunk to the ocean floor. Survivors in lifeboats and life jackets may have been carried far away from the scene by the ocean's current.

For instance, rescue workers found nothing when they arrived to help victims of the *Pride of Baltimore*. This ship sank near Puerto Rico in 1986. Rescue workers had to search for four days to find the survivors, who were floating in life jackets.

COAST GUARDS

In many countries, coast guards carry out search-and-rescue missions. Years ago, coast guards really were guards. These people stood guard onshore, especially during stormy weather. These guards watched for ships that were running aground in the bad weather. Then the guards rowed rescue boats out to the scene to help the shipwreck victims.

Modern coast guards are much different. The U.S. Coast Guard, for instance, is part of the military. It has ships, airplanes, helicopters, and thousands of workers. Members of the U.S. Coast Guard have rescued thousands of people.

A small boat rescues a man from the water after the
USS *West Virginia* was bombed in the Japanese
attack on Pearl Harbor on December 7, 1941.

RESCUE AT SEA

The U.S. Coast Guard and coast guards of other countries have specially equipped airplanes and helicopters to search for disaster victims. Once the victims are located, more helicopters arrive to begin the rescue.

A U.S. Coast Guard helicopter brings equipment to stranded tourists on a ship near Alaska.

Helicopters hover (stay in one spot) over the water. Helicopter crews drop life rafts or life preservers to people in the water. A helicopter also may pull disaster victims up out of the water.

UP, UP, AND AWAY!

Search-and-rescue helicopters come equipped with long cables that can be lowered to a person in the water. The cable may have a sling or a chairlike basket attached to one end. The survivor puts his or her arms through the sling or climbs into the basket.

Then the cable is pulled back up. The survivor rises up through the air. The coast guard crew helps that person into the helicopter. The helicopter pilot then flies the survivor to safety and medical attention.

Coast guards also have powerful rescue ships. These ships can sail safely through the stormiest water. They speed to a disaster scene and pick up the survivors. The survivors then receive medical care on board the ship, until they can be taken to a hospital on land.

FAMILIES AND FRIENDS

The families and friends of survivors and victims also need help. First, they need information. Relatives may learn about a disaster from the television, radio, or Internet. They will be scared and desperate for information. Have their loved ones been rescued? Are they alive? Are they dead?

"No one is telling us anything," Shaaban el Qott said. His cousin was on the *Al-Salam Boccaccio 98* when it sank in 2006. "All I want to know [is] if he's dead or alive."

A helicopter rescues passengers from a burning ferry during a practice rescue operation in Seoul, South Korea, in 2007.

CRISIS CENTERS

Relief workers help provide information to families and friends of disaster victims. Workers often set up a crisis center after a disaster at sea. The center is a building or other place where relatives can wait for news. It is staffed with specially trained workers.

The Red Cross and Red Crescent are international organizations that help to relieve suffering caused by disasters. These organizations often provide the specially trained workers. Part of the workers' job involves giving psychological support to victims' relatives. "Some of those waiting for information were hysterical," said Aziz Diop, a Red Crescent worker who helped victims' families after the *Joola* ferry sank in 2002.

RECOVERING BODIES

Work at a disaster scene continues long after all the survivors are taken to safety. Rescue workers try to recover the bodies of the people who died in the disaster. When the *Estonia* sank, for instance, divers went deep under the Baltic Sea to search for the dead.

Doctors, counselors, and others who can give emotional help to rescue workers also work at crisis centers. These workers see terrible things. They see dead bodies. Sometimes the bodies have been partially eaten by fish. The workers have to pull the bodies from the water. Talking to someone with expert training may help rescue workers cope with their feelings.

REMEMBERING THE VICTIMS

When a person dies, his or her loved ones are very sad. They grieve by crying and remembering the person who has died. Expressing their sadness helps people accept their loss. It helps them continue with their own lives.

Grieving is easier if the dead person's body can be returned to the family. The body helps family members accept that their loved one is dead. Family members may express grief at funeral services in houses of worship. Or they may conduct memorial services in a house of worship, outdoors, or in some other place. Services such as these are part of recovering from a devastating loss.

Men wait to identify bodies of relatives who were on board the *Al-Salam Boccaccio 98* ferry when it sank on February 2, 2006.

"*It was horrible, because we were hearing people screaming from underneath.*"

—Moussa Ndong, a passenger on board the Joola

A raft sits to the left of the capsized ferryboat *Joola* on September 27, 2002. Rescuers dropped life rafts into the water for possible survivors of the accident in the Atlantic Ocean.

September 26, 2002
THE *JOOLA* DISASTER

People in the African country of Senegal often take ferryboats to travel between the northern and southern parts of the country because the nation of Gambia separates them. Guards at the border of Gambia stop everyone traveling by road. The guards check to see why those people are traveling. That makes travel by road very slow.

On September 26, 2002, almost 2,000 people crowded onto the ferry *Joola*. They were going from southern Senegal to the country's capital city, Dakar. The *Joola*, however, was built to carry only 550 people.

When a boat is overloaded, it floats deeper in the water. That makes it easier for waves in a storm to wash onto the deck. A few hours after sailing, the overloaded *Joola* was 21 miles (34 km) off the coast of Gambia.

There it met a storm. Strong winds blew water onto the deck. Heavy rain poured more water into the ship. Suddenly, passengers noticed that the *Joola* was tipping to the left. It tipped even farther.

"Everything happened so quickly," said Moulay Badgi, a passenger on the *Joola*. *"The boat overturned in less than 5 minutes. I heard the crying of the children and it was terrible."*

As the *Joola* tipped to one side, some passengers jumped off. However, many could not escape before the boat capsized. People on the *Joola's* deck were under the water.

Cheikh Niang remembered a flood of water as the *Joola* turned upside down. He swam out through an open window. *"The sea was really choppy [rough] and cold,"* he said.

"It was horrible, because we were hearing people screaming from underneath," said another passenger, Moussa Ndong. Moussa and other survivors clung to the side of the boat. Others climbed on top of the capsized boat. *"I survived,"* said Patrice Auvray. *"But I saw my wife drown and I could do nothing to help."*

Ben Badji and many other passengers, however, had to struggle to stay afloat in the ocean. *"After the boat capsized, we were thrown about by the wind and huge waves until about four in the morning."* Then he floated close to the boat and clung to one side.

Finally, fishing boats arrived at the disaster scene and rescued Ben and the other survivors. Nobody is sure how many people died when this disaster struck. Some people believe there were eighteen hundred deaths.

Fishing boats surround the capsized *Joola* (below left) in an attempt to rescue survivors on September 27, 2002. Rescue workers had to rush to find survivors and to retrieve the dead before the ferry sank to the bottom of the Atlantic Ocean (below right).

Measuring a Menace

WHEN A DISASTER AT SEA HAPPENS, PEOPLE ASK QUESTIONS. HOW BAD WAS THE DISASTER? HOW MANY PEOPLE WERE KILLED? HOW MANY WERE INJURED? THE ANSWERS TELL ABOUT THE SEVERITY OF THE DISASTER.

In that way, one disaster at sea can be compared to another. Those comparisons are important. They help us remember the worst disasters and teach us lessons to help us avoid other disasters from occurring.

FINDING OUT WHY

Even more important, however, is measuring the "why" of a disaster. We must know the reason each disaster happened. That information can make us aware of safety problems on a ship. Then engineers can fix those problems. Correcting those problems can save lives. Other ships of the same kind may have similar safety problems. If those problems are not fixed, they could cause another disaster.

THE TIP OF A SHIP

In 2006 a cruise ship named the *Crown Princess* was near Florida. About forty-three hundred people were on board. The *Crown Princess* suddenly tipped to one side. When the ship tipped, people were thrown around. "All the water from the [ship's swimming] pools was coming right over the edge," said passenger Alfred Caproni. "It was like Niagara Falls."

About 240 passengers suffered cuts, broken bones, and other injuries. Finding out why the ship tipped partway over is important. If a serious problem exists, it might get worse on that ship or other ships.

The *Crown Princess* returns to port at Cape Canaveral, Florida, on July 18, 2006. The cruise ship suddenly tilted to one side while at sea, and more than two hundred passengers were injured.

Someday, a passenger ship might tip even farther to the side. It might tip all the way over and sink. And if it happens far out at sea, thousands of passengers may drown. (By early 2008, the cause of the *Crown Princess* incident was still being investigated.)

DISASTER DETECTIVES

Specially trained people investigate disasters on water. In the United States, some of those people work for the National Transportation Safety Board (NTSB). This government agency is in Washington, D.C. Investigators from the

Victims of the *Empress of Ireland (top)* and *Neptune* disasters *(bottom)*

FORGOTTEN DISASTERS

A disaster with a death toll almost as high as the *Titanic*'s occurred in May 1914, just two years after the *Titanic* disaster. The *Empress of Ireland*, a ship with 1,477 passengers and crew, collided with a coal ship on the Saint Lawrence River in Canada, killing 1,012 people.

People forgot about the sinking of the *Empress of Ireland* because a bigger event— World War I (1914–1918)—broke out a few months later.

In 1993 a ferryboat called the *Neptune* sank in the Caribbean Sea near Haiti during a storm. The death toll in this disaster was about seventeen hundred people—two hundred more than the *Titanic*. The sinking of the *Neptune*, however, failed to capture the public's attention as much as the *Titanic*'s sinking.

"When *I opened my eyes* [in the water] *I could not imagine where I was* or what had happened, and then I lifted my head and saw a deck chair under me and all around me were **dead bodies floating.**"

—Margaret Greenaway, Empress of Ireland survivor, 1914

National Transportation Safety Board inspectors examine a submarine after it collided with a Japanese boat in February 2001.

NTSB work to discover the cause of disasters on water so that safety problems on ships and boats can be corrected. Often, after the cause of a disaster is determined, the NTSB suggests new safety rules to prevent future disasters.

People from the U.S. Coast Guard also investigate sea disasters. After a disaster, the coast guard checks to see if the ship had been following safety rules. If the ship broke rules, the coast guard might arrest the captain or shipowner.

BLACK BOXES

When a disaster happens, a "Go Team" from the NTSB hurries to the scene. The team studies the ship. They look for evidence, such as holes in the hull, that may have caused the disaster. Go Teams interview eyewitnesses. They also check information recorded in a ship's voyage data recorder (VDR).

Many large cruise ships have a VDR. Also called black boxes, VDRs are similar to flight data recorders on airplanes. VDRs record what the ship was doing just before the disaster. They tell about changes in the ship's speed, for instance, and direction.

PUTTING THE PIECES TOGETHER

The NTSB uses all the information, plus weather records and radar or sonar data, to investigate the disaster. It is almost like the investigation that police use to solve a crime. Investigating a disaster on water may be very difficult. A ship may not have a VDR, for instance. There may be no eyewitnesses because everyone died in the disaster. As a result, some NTSB investigations can take years to complete.

When the investigation is complete, the NTSB investigators write a report. That report explains how the disaster happened. The report also may suggest safety improvements to prevent future disasters.

The cruise ship *Sea Diamond* is evacuated near Greece in April 2007. The ship began to sink after it ran aground on the rocky coast.

The *Ethan Allen* tour boat is brought to the surface of Lake George, in New York, on October 3, 2005.

october 2, 2005
THE *ETHAN ALLEN*

Passengers boarded the *Ethan Allen* on a picture-perfect day. This tour boat took people sightseeing on Lake George in upstate New York. The lake was calm. There was almost no wind. The water looked as smooth as glass. Bright sun was shining from a clear blue sky.

The *Ethan Allen* filled up quickly with forty-seven passengers and the captain. The passengers were senior citizens. These elderly people were on a tour to see the beautiful autumn leaves in the mountains surrounding the lake. Two people on the tour, however, decided not to ride on the boat. They thought it was too crowded.

However, the captain wasn't worried about overloading the boat. He knew that the *Ethan Allen* could safely hold fifty passengers.

Everyone was enjoying the cruise. Suddenly, the *Ethan Allen* began rocking back and forth. **"Whoop-dee-doo,"** joked one passenger. **"I love rocking the boat."** The *Ethan Allen* tipped sideways to the right. Then it tipped to the left. It kept on tipping and flipped over into the water.

"We had joked . . . [that] there were too many people on the left because

the boat was listing," said passenger Jean Siler. *"As the boat was making a turn, I saw water was coming over the left side."* Anna May Hawley remembered what happened next. *"People started sliding off their benches and the boat kept [tipping sideways] and flipped right over,"* she said.

Carol Charlton slid off her seat as the boat tipped. *"[T]hen I was in the black water and I knew I was under the boat. I cannot swim and I remember . . . pushing myself up. I saw light. Then I surfaced and clung to the boat with several other people. The boat was upside down."* Many of the other passengers could not swim. However, they were not as lucky as Charlton. Twenty passengers drowned in Lake George, which was 70 feet (21 m) deep.

After the disaster, people realized something about the rule that allowed the *Ethan Allen* to carry fifty passengers. The rule was made in 1960. In those days, the average person weighed 145 pounds (66 kg).

People have gotten heavier since then. In 2005 the average man weighed 191 pounds (87 kg). The average woman weighed 164 pounds (74 kg). Even with just forty-seven passengers, the boat was overloaded.

With too much weight on board, the boat floated deeper in the water. Water spilled over onto the boat's deck. As water collected on the left side of the boat, it tipped sideways farther and farther until it tipped over.

Another boat helps pull the *Ethan Allen* to the surface in October 2005.

47

The Future

DISASTERS ON WATER OFTEN TEACH IMPORTANT LESSONS. THEY MAKE US AWARE OF SAFETY PROBLEMS ON SHIPS, FOR INSTANCE. BY CORRECTING THOSE PROBLEMS, WE MAY PREVENT FUTURE DISASTERS.

We have learned lessons from old disasters, such as the *Titanic*. People on that ship died because there were not enough lifeboats on board. And some of those boats could not be launched because it was too hard to get them off the deck.

After that disaster, passenger ships began carrying more lifeboats. New laws required shipowners to carry enough lifeboats for every passenger on a ship. More efficient designs of the lifeboats made them easier to put into the water.

Modern disasters continue teaching us lessons. We learned from the *Ethan Allen* disaster in 2005. Rules said the *Ethan Allen* could safely carry fifty people. But those rules were forty-five years old. The *Ethan Allen* disaster made people realize that weight-limit rules needed to be updated.

FLOATING CITIES

Large cruise ships are almost like small towns. They carry thousands of passengers. These ships often have restaurants, shops, and movie theaters. They have day care centers, health clubs, and hospitals.

Like cities, cruise ships also have their own emergency services. They have fire departments, for instance, and emergency medical teams. The crew members who are specially trained for these jobs can help keep a ship from sinking. If a ship does sink, crew members can save lives by helping passengers escape.

Lifeboats from the *Titanic* float at dock after passengers were rescued from them. The lack of an adequate number of lifeboats contributed to the high death toll when the *Titanic* sank on April 14, 1912

ENFORCING OLD RULES

Future disasters may be prevented by enforcing rules that already exist. When the *Al-Salam Boccaccia 98* sank in 2006, Egypt already had laws that required ships to carry enough lifeboats for all the passengers. But the *Al-Salam* was breaking the rule. Nobody made sure that the boat followed the rules. Many other disasters on water happened because people broke the rules.

Other ferryboat operators broke the rules and carried too many passengers. The operators also broke the rules by not carrying enough life jackets. Enforcing those rules could have saved thousands of lives.

MAKING NEW RULES

One new rule may be especially important in preventing future disasters at sea. In 2006 the NTSB said stricter rules are needed to prevent crews from using drugs or alcohol during work hours. Using these substances can make people behave dangerously.

SEA MONSTERS

Sea monsters can cause disasters for modern-day ships. But these "monsters" are actually huge waves called rogue waves. Rogue waves appear without warning. Some are more than 100 feet (30 m) high. In 2005 a 70-foot (21 m) rogue wave almost caused a disaster for the *Norwegian Dawn*. That cruise ship was in the Atlantic Ocean off the coast of Georgia. The wave smashed windows, flooded rooms, and frightened the passengers and crew. "The ship was like a cork in a bathtub," said passenger Celestine Mcelhatton. Later, the ship reached shore safely.

That behavior can be especially dangerous on ships. The NTSB said that better drug testing was one of the most important steps needed to improve safety on ships. In the past, crews often were not tested properly for drug or alcohol abuse after an accident.

Without proper testing, some crew members thought they could use drugs without getting caught. Drug and alcohol testing is important for another reason. It helps safety officials find out how often drug abusers cause disasters on water. Then new rules are made to ensure that drug abusers aren't working on boats or ships.

The cruise ship *Norwegian Dawn* was hit by a rogue wave off the coast of Georgia in 2005.

LESS SEARCH . . .

In the future, better automatic distress signaling devices could save lives. These devices could take some of the "search" out of search and rescue. Future devices may be small and very inexpensive.

The signaling devices could be put on every lifeboat. They also could be built into every life preserver. Distress signals of the future may be stronger. This means they could be more accurate in showing the location of disaster victims. As a result, rescue teams may spend less time looking for survivors. And the rescue teams may be able to find more survivors to rescue.

MORE RESCUE

Newly designed rescue boats may allow help to arrive faster at the scene of a disaster. In the past, stormy weather and high waves sometimes delayed rescuers. Future rescue boats may be like the U.S. Coast Guard's Motor Lifeboats.

These amazing boats are 47 feet (14 m) long. They can sail at 29 miles (46 km) per hour when waves are up to 30 feet (9 m) high. Those waves would reach the top of a three-story building.

Waves may tip the Motor Lifeboat upside down. However, the Motor Lifeboat is designed to float like a cork. It automatically turns upright again within eight seconds.

In the future, ships may carry small Motor Lifeboats. When disaster strikes a nearby ship, the Motor Lifeboats could speed to the scene to aid in rescuing survivors.

FORGOTTEN INVENTOR

Lionel Lukin of Great Britain is today credited for inventing the first lifeboat in 1784. He started with a 20-foot-long (6 m) wooden boat. Lukin put cork inside the hull of the boat to make it float better. He made other improvements that kept the boat from sinking in rough water. Lukin tried to convince the British navy to put lifeboats on warships. Nobody listened, however. Only after the *Titanic* disaster in 1912 did laws require a sufficient number of lifeboats on passenger ships.

This boat on a
ferry is used for
rescue work.

AN UNSINKABLE SHIP?

When the *Titanic* sank in 1912, so did the idea of an unsinkable ship. *Titanic* had been called unsinkable. That ship had a twin called the *Britannic*. After the *Titanic* disaster, workers made changes to the *Britannic*. Those changes made the ship safer. In 1916, however, the *Britannic* sank within an hour of being hit by a torpedo or a mine while serving as a hospital ship off the coast of Greece during World War I.

The lesson from these and other ships is that no ship is unsinkable. In the future, engineers will try to build boats and ships that are nearly unsinkable, however. The Motor Lifeboat is one such vessel. Improvements to this and other boats and ships will improve safety for all passengers and crew. The chances of disasters occurring will be lowered.

The wreckage of the *Titanic* on the ocean floor near Newfoundland, Canada, is a reminder of the importance of safety at sea.

NO-SCARE SAILING

Horrible disasters have happened at sea. Thousands of people have been killed and injured. Disasters at sea, however, are actually quite rare.

Each year, millions of people sail safely on cruise ships, ferryboats, sightseeing boats, and other kinds of boats. Ships and boats are a very safe way to travel. Don't let worries about disasters on water spoil the fun of sailing. By following a few safety rules, you can travel even more safely.

SAFETY RULES

Disasters on water can happen suddenly. Here are some tips for cruise ship passengers:

- Be sure to participate in the ship's fire and lifeboat drills. These practice sessions show passengers what to do in an emergency at sea.

- Each cabin has a poster containing emergency instructions. You can find it on the wall or the cabin door. When you first board the ship, take a few minutes to read the instructions. The instructions will tell you how to recognize the ship's emergency signals (bells and whistles).

- Each cabin has its own life preservers. Read the instructions and pictures that explain how to put on a life preserver. Make sure you understand how to adjust the straps.

- Find out which lifeboat to use in an emergency. Then take a few minutes to walk to that lifeboat so you can find it quickly in an emergency. Direction signs should be posted in the ship's passageways and stairways.

- If you don't understand any instructions, ask a crew member to explain them to you. Keep asking questions until you get clear answers that you fully understand.

- If there is an emergency, stay calm. Listen for announcements and instructions on the ship's public-address system. If there are no announcements, follow the instructions from the poster in your cabin and the drills you have participated in.

- Once you are safely off the ship, try to stay as dry as possible. If you are in the water, swim to a lifeboat. Remember that you can freeze to death in very cold water.

There may be no safety drills or instructions on ferries and other small boats. Look for emergency instructions posted on a wall. If necessary, ask a crew member where to find life preservers. Ask about lifeboats or life rafts. Ask what to do in an emergency.

Timeline

1865 The steamboat *Sultana* explodes in the Mississippi River, killing 1,700 Union soldiers.

1878 The British ship *Princess Alice* collides with the Bywell Castle on the River Thames. About 700 people drown.

1904 The steamship *General Slocum*, on a Sunday picnic excursion, catches fire in the East River in New York, and 1,200 people die.

1912 The world's largest luxury passenger steamship, the *Titanic (above)*, sinks after hitting an iceberg. More than 1,500 people die.

1914 Fog causes a fatal accident on the Saint Lawrence River in Canada when the *Empress of Ireland* collides with the coal freighter *Storstad (below)*. More than 1,000 people drown.

1915 Western Electric Company employees, on their way to their annual picnic, crowd aboard the *Eastland*, anchored in the Chicago River. The *Eastland* capsizes, and 844 people drown.

1916 During World War I, the French ship *Provence* is sunk by a German submarine in the Mediterranean Sea. Approximately 3,100 people are killed.

1940 A German bomb hits the *Lancastria*, a British troopship carrying approximately 7,000 sailors, soldiers, and civilians. More than 4,000 people are killed.

1941 On September 18, a British submarine torpedoes two Italian military transport ships, the *Neptunia* and the *Oceania*. Approximately 5,000 people drown.

1944 The Japanese ship *Junyo Maru* sinks after being torpedoed by a British submarine. More than 5,000 prisoners of war are killed. The same year, a U.S. submarine torpedoes the Japanese ship, *Toyama Maru*, killing 5,400.

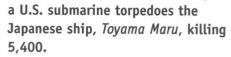
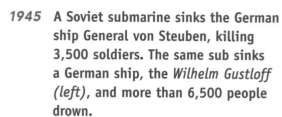

1945 A Soviet submarine sinks the German ship General von Steuben, killing 3,500 soldiers. The same sub sinks a German ship, the *Wilhelm Gustloff (left)*, and more than 6,500 people drown.

1948 A Chinese ship evacuating troops sinks off the coast of China, killing 6,000 people.

1954 A typhoon sinks five Japanese passenger ships, including the *Toya Maru*, killing a total of 1,430 people.

1987 The overcrowded ferry *Doña Paz (right)* collides with the tanker *Victor* in the Philippines. The resulting fire creates panic, and 4,340 people drown.

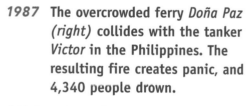

1994 A storm in the Baltic Sea causes the ferry *Estonia* to sink *(below)*, killing 852 people.

2002 The ferry *Joola* is destroyed in a storm, killing approximately 1,800 people.

2003 High winds cause a ferryboat in Staten Island, New York, to crash into a pier, killing ten passengers and injuring thirty-four.

2006 The Egyptian ferry *Al-Salam Boccaccio 98*, carrying 1,400 people, sinks in the Red Sea.

Glossary

capsize: to turn upside down

crisis center: a place where people can obtain information and emotional support

Emergency Position-Indicating Radio Beacon (EPIRB): an electronic device that sends out a distress signal

ferry: a boat that carries people back and forth between two ports on a regular schedule

hull: the sides, bottom, and deck of a ship or boat

hypothermia: low body temperature that can make a person freeze to death

International Morse Code: the system that uses signals that consist of either dots and dashes or long and short sounds to transmit messages

lifeboat: a rigid or inflatable boat used to rescue people

Motor Lifeboat: an almost unsinkable boat used for rescues in rough water

recreational boats: small boats that people sail for fun

ships: large vehicles for traveling over water. Ships may carry their own small boats, such as lifeboats

submarine: a ship designed to travel underwater

voyage data recorder (VDR): an electronic device (also called a black box) that records information about a ship. The information can be used to identify the cause of a disaster.

Places to Visit

The Mariner's Museum—Newport News, Virginia
http://www.mariner.org/visitorinfo
See exhibits of famous ships and submarines, as well as models of steamships, and learn about the role of the navy in U.S. history.

The Musee de la Mer—Rimouski, Quebec, Canada
http://www.museedelamer.qc.ca/en
At this museum, you can learn about the history of the *Empress of Ireland*, which sank in the Saint Lawrence River in May 1914.

Mystic Seaport—Mystic, Connecticut
http://www.mysticseaport.org
This village is known as the Museum of America and the Sea. You can visit a re-created nineteenth-century seaport village, learn about ships and ship restorations, and view films about the sea and famous shipwrecks.

Shipwreck Historeum—Key West, Florida
http://www.shipwreckhistoreum.com
Stop in at this history museum and find out what it is like to be rescued from sinking ships.

Source Notes

4   Nadir Jalal Abd al-Shafi, quoted in "Captain Was First to Flee, Say Survivors," February 4, 2006, http://english.aljazeera.net/NR/exeres/D0ABA196-CC68-4C93-A336-A3592A087C0D.htm (February 5, 2006).

4   Abdul Rahman, quoted in Daniel Williams, "Captain Refused Action to Thwart Ferry Disaster," *Washington Post*, February 5, 2006.

4   Nazih Zaki, quoted in Mona el-Naggar and Hassan M. Fattah, "Only 400 Rescued as Blame Shifts to Sunken Ship's Captain," *International Herald Tribune*, February 5, 2006, http://www.iht.com/articles/2006/02/05/news/ship.php (June 18, 2007).

5   Ahmed Elew, quoted in Associated Press, "Ferry with 1,400 Aboard Sinks; Most Feared Dead," *USA Today*, February 3, 2006, http://www.usatoday.com/news/world/2006-02-03-egypt-cruise_x.htm?POE=NEWISVA (June 18, 2007).

5   Ibid.

5   Salah Jomaa, quoted in "Egypt Not Told for Hours That Ferry Sank: He Was Acting as If We Were Not Human," February 8, 2006, http://web.archive.org/web/20060308124717/http://www.cnn.com/2006/WORLD/meast/02/07/egypt.ferry.ap/index.html (June 12, 2006).

6   Kent Harstedt, quoted in S-G. Berglund, "Estonia: Some Facts from the Disaster," April 10, 1994, http://www.kolumbus.fi/estonia/estonia5.html (June 16, 2007).

9   Haidar el Ali, quoted in Jamey Keaten, "Divers Reveal Horrors of Accident," *Daily Texan Online*, October 1, 2002, http://www.dailytexanonline.com/media/storage/paper410/news/2002/10/01/WorldNation/Divers.Reveal.Horrors.Of.Accident (June 19, 2006).

10 James Robert Collins, quoted in "J. R. Collins Tells of the Sinking of the Sultana: Civil War Reminiscence," *Plainville (KS) Times*, May 28, 1908, http://www.couchgenweb.com/civilwar/sultana.htm (May 27, 2006).

11 Ibid.

11 William H. Norton, quoted in Mark J. Price, "Forgotten Maritime Disaster Killed Troops Returning from War," *Akron (OH) Beacon Journal*, April 26, 2003.

11 Arthur A. Jones, quoted in Mark J. Price, "Forgotten Maritime Disaster Killed Troops Returning from War."

11 William H. Norton, quoted in Mark J. Price, "Forgotten Maritime Disaster Killed Troops Returning from War."

11 Unnamed passenger, quoted in Cedric A. Larson, "Death on the Dark River," *American Heritage 6*, no. 6 (1955).

11 James Robert Collins, quoted in "J. R. Collins Tells of the Sinking of the Sultana: Civil War Reminiscence."

14 Thomas Thorn, quoted in Bob Kriebel, "Sultana Survivors Recall Tribulations," *Lafayette (IN) Journal and Courier*, June 23, 2002.

19 Arnel Galang, quoted in Eileen Guerrero, "Misery Haunts Survivor of Major Ship Disaster," *Houston Chronicle*, December 19, 1988.

21 Mrs. Peter Reniff, quoted in "Elizabeth Woman, *Titanic* Survivor, Tells of Tragedy," *Elizabeth (NJ) Daily Journal*, April 19, 1912, http://www.encyclopediatitanica.org/print/2455 (July 22, 2006).

21 Ruth Becker, quoted in Jennifer Kirkpatrick, "I Survived the Titanic," *National Geographic Kids*, July 1996, http://www.nationalgeographic.com/ngkids/9607/titanic.html (June 18, 2007).

21 Washington Dodge, quoted in "San Francisco Assessor Tells Story of the Wreck of the Titanic from Which He Escapes after Thrilling Experience," *San Francisco Bulletin*, April 19, 1912, http://www.sfmuseum.org/hist5/dodge.html (July 22, 2006).

21 Ruth Becker, quoted in Jennifer Kirkpatrick, "I Survived the *Titanic*."

21 Ibid.

27 Einar Kukk, quoted in Stefan Lundberg and Greg Mcivor, "Sound of Silence Signals Catastrophe," *Guardian* (London), September 29, 1994.

27 Tom Johansson, quoted in "Terror of Passengers Too Weak to Save Themselves," *Times* (London), September 30, 1994.

27 Carl Oevberg, quoted in "Terror of Passengers Too Weak to Save Themselves."

27 Paul Barney, quoted in Jon Ungoed-Thomas, "I Saved #12 and It Saved My Life," *Scottish Daily Record* (Glasgow), September 30, 1994.

27 Carl Oevberg, quoted in "Terror of Passengers Too Weak to Save Themselves."

31 Kaichiki Yamakazi, quoted in Stephen J. Spignesi, *The 100 Greatest Disasters of All Time* (New York: Kensington Publishing, 2002), page 165.

34 Shaaban el Qott, quoted in "Series of Tragic Errors Doomed Egypt Ferry," February 4, 2006, http://wcbstv.com/national/topstories_story_035091017.html (June 18, 2007).

36 Aziz Diop, quoted in Jessica Barry, "Senegal Ferry Disaster Reveals Need for Psychological Support," *International Federation of Red Cross and Red Crescent Societies*, March 3, 2003.

38 Moussa Ndong, quoted in "Hopes Fade in Senegal Ferry Search," BBC News, September 28, 2002, http://news.bbc.co.uk/1/hi/world/africa/2288376.stm (July 4, 2006).

39 Moulay Badgi, quoted in "Hopes Fade in Senegal Ferry Search," BBC News, September 28, 2002, http://news.bbc.co.uk/1/hi/world/africa/2288376.stm (July 4, 2006).

39 Cheikh Niang, quoted in "Hopes Fade in Senegal Ferry Search," BBC News, September 28, 2002, http://news.bbc.co.uk/1/hi/world/africa/2288376.stm (July 4, 2006).

39 Moussa Ndong, quoted in "Hopes Fade in Senegal Ferry Search."

39 Patrice Auvray, quoted in "Hopes Fade in Senegal Ferry Search," BBC News, September 28, 2002, http://news.bbc.co.uk/1/hi/world/africa/2288376.stm (July 4, 2006).

39 Ben Badji, quoted in "Hopes Fade in Senegal Ferry Search," BBC News, September 28, 2002, http://news.bbc.co.uk/1/hi/world/africa/2288376.stm (July 4, 2006).

40 Alfred Caproni, quoted in Maria Newman, "New Cruise Ship Lists Unexpectedly," *New York Times*, July 19, 2006.

43 Margaret Greenaway, transcript of letter to her husband's parents, 1914, http://www1.salvationarmy.org/heritage.nsf (June 19, 2006).

46 Unnamed passenger, quoted in Candace Choi, "Thrashing, Screaming and Heroism during Boat Tragedy on New York Lake," *Detroit News*, October 3, 2005.

46–47 Jean Siler, report on *Ethan Allen* accident, Warren County (NY) Sheriff's Office, Incident No. 2005–13724.

47 Anna May Hawley, report on *Ethan Allen* accident.

47 Carol Charlton, report on *Ethan Allen* accident.

47 Hawley, report on *Ethan Allen* accident.

50 Celestine Mcelhatton, quoted in William J. Broad, "Rogue Giants at Sea," *New York Times*, April 16, 2005.

Selected Bibliography

Bonner, Kit, and Carolyn Bonner. *Great Ship Disasters*. Saint Paul: MBI Publishing, 2003.

Brandt, Anthony, ed. *The Tragic History of the Sea*. New York: Random House, 2006.

Davis, Lee. *Man Made Disasters*. New York: Facts On File. 2002.

Flayhart, William. *Perils of the Atlantic: Steamship Disasters, 1850 to the Present*. New York: W. W. Norton & Company, 2003.

Konstam, Angus. *The History of Shipwrecks*. New York: Lyons Press, 1999.

Krieger, Michael. *All the Men in the Sea: The Untold Story of One of the Greatest Rescues in History*. New York: Free Press, 2002.

Lawrence, Richard Russell, ed. *The Mammoth Book of Storms, Shipwrecks and Sea Disasters*. New York: Carroll & Graff Publishers, 2004.

Ritchie, David. *Shipwrecks: An Encyclopedia of the World's Worst Disasters at Sea*. New York: Facts On File, 1996.

Spignesi, Stephen J. *The 100 Greatest Disasters of All Time*. New York: Kensington Publishing, 2002.

Willis, Clint. *Rough Waters: Stories of Survival from the Sea*. New York: Thunder's Mouth Press, 1999.

Wise, James E., Jr. *Sole Survivors of the Sea*. Baltimore: Nautical and Aviation Publishing Company of America, 1994.

Zine, David. *Forgotten Empress: The Empress of Ireland Story*. Tiverton, UK: Halsgrove Publishing, 1998.

Further Resources

BOOKS

Autio, Karen. *Second Watch*. Winlaw, BC: Sono Nis Press, 2005.
In this novel, Saara, eleven, and her mother are traveling to Finland on the doomed *Empress of Ireland* in 1914 when it collides with a coal ship on the Saint Lawrence River in Canada.

Ballard, Robert. *Ghost Liners: Exploring the World's Greatest Lost Ships*. Boston: Madison Press / Little Brown, 1998.
Find out more about the *Britannic*, the *Empress of Ireland*, the *Titanic*, and other ship disasters.

Leroe, Ellen. *Disaster: Three Real-Life Stories of Survival*. New York: Hyperion Books, 2000.
This is the story of the sinking of the Canadian Pacific liner *Empress of Ireland*, as told from the viewpoint of two of the survivors.

McMurray, Kevin F. *Dark Descent: Diving and the Deadly Allure of the* Empress of Ireland. New York: McGraw-Hill, 2004.

The *Empress of Ireland* sank into the Saint Lawrence River in fourteen minutes. McMurray recounts his exploits in visiting the wrecked vessel.

Rousmaniere, John. *After the Storm: True Stories of Disaster and Recovery at Sea*. New York: McGraw Hill, 2002.

Sailors have always been in harm's way on the sea. This book tells of storm experiences and survival stories on various types of sea vessels.

Sandler, Martin. *America's Great Disasters*. New York: HarperCollins, 2003.

Sandler writes about the tragedy of the *Sultana* and how Americans recovered from the disaster.

White, Ellen Emerson. *Voyage of the Great Titanic: The Diary of Margaret Ann Brady, R.M.S. Titanic, 1912*. New York: Scholastic, 1998.

In this novel, Margaret Ann longs to reunite with her brother in the United States and receives the opportunity when she is hired as a ladies' companion on the maiden voyage of the *Titanic*.

Woods, Michael, and Mary B. Woods. *Fires*. Minneapolis: Lerner Publications Company, 2007.

Find out about what happened on the *General Slocum* steamboat, when a church picnic turned into a tragedy.

WEB SITES AND FILMS

The Online Titanic Museum
http://www.onlinetitanicmuseum.com/
This is a fascinating online exhibit of memorabilia from the *Titanic*.

Savage Seas: Surviving in Stormy Seas
http://www.thirteen.org/savageseas/captain-main.html
The Public Broadcasting Service (PBS) maintains this site on surviving the savage sea. Here you can hear Anders Ericson's story of surviving the sinking of the ferry *Estonia*, and more.

Some Shipwrecks and Disasters at Sea
http://home.cc.umanitoba.ca/~wyatt/wrecks.html
This site includes a treasure trove of statistics on people who have lost their lives at sea.

The United States Coast Guard: Department of Homeland Security
http://www.uscg.mil/USCG.shtm
Here you'll find everything about this branch of the military that works to prevent disasters at sea and assist victims when disasters strike.

U.S. Navy Computerized Shipwreck Database
http://prosea.org/articles-news/exploration/US_Navy_Computerized_Shipwreck_Database.html
At this site, the U.S. Navy provides information on almost every known shipwreck.

Lost Ships of the Mediterranean. DVD. Washington, DC: National Geographic Society, 2000.

Undersea adventurer Robert Ballard and his team explore the remains of some of the oldest shipwrecks in the world, including one from biblical times.

Titanic: The Complete Story. DVD. New York: History Channel, 2001.

Listen to survivor stories about the sinking of the *Titanic*.

Unsolved History: Wilhelm Gustloff—Deadliest Sea Disaster. DVD. Silver Spring, MD: Discovery Channel, 2003.

Discover some secrets about this disaster that claimed more than six thousand lives.

Index

Photo Acknowledgments

The photographs in this book are used with the permission of: AP Photo/Xinhua, Li Jianshu, p. 1; © Photodisc/ Getty Images, pp. 1 (background), all borders; © Wilfried Krecichwost/zefa/Corbis, p. 3; © Hassan Ammar/ AFP/Getty Images, pp. 4, 29; AP Photo/Yvon Perchoc, p. 5; © EP TravelStock/Alamy, p. 7; AP Photo/Aaron Jackson, p. 8; AP Photo/HO, French Navy, pp. 9, 38, 39 (both); Library of Congress, pp. 10 (LC-USZ62-77201), 11 (LC-USZ62-48778), 42 top (LC-DIG-ggbain-18100); © Peter Macdiarmid/Getty Images, p. 13; AP Photo/ Ricardo Mazalan, p. 15; AP Photo, pp. 16, 19, 23, 27, 57 (middle); AP Photo/Thomas Haentzschel, p. 17; © SuperStock, Inc./SuperStock , p. 20; AP Photo/Frank O. Braynard Collection, p. 21; AP Photo/Heinz Ducklau, p. 22; © Bill Hauser/Independent Picture Service, pp. 24–25; AP Photo/Veikko Wahlroos, p. 26; © Naum Chayer/Alamy, p. 31; Courtesy ACR Electronics, Inc., p. 32; © Bettmann/CORBIS, p. 33; © Craig Lovell/CORBIS, p. 34; © Jeon Young-Han/AFP/Getty Images, p. 35; © Khaled Desouki/AFP/Getty Images, p. 37; AP Photo/John Raoux, p. 41; © Thony Belizaire/AFP/Getty Images, p. 42 (bottom); © Mai/Time Life Pictures/Getty Images, p. 43; © AFP/Getty Images, p. 45; AP Photo/Mary Altaffer, pp. 46, 47; © The Print Collector/Alamy, p. 49; © Norman Wharton/Alamy, p. 51; © Greg Gilman/Alamy, p. 53; © Ralph White/CORBIS, p. 54; © Pacific Stock/SuperStock, p. 55; ullstein bild/The Granger Collection, New York, p. 56 (top); © Hulton Archive/Getty Images, p. 56 (bottom); © Hugo Jaeger/Time Life Pictures/Getty Images, p. 57 (top); AP Photo/Jaakko Avikainen, p. 57 (bottom).

Front cover: © Amiel Meneses/epa/Corbis

Back cover: © Photodisc/Getty Images

About the Authors

Michael Woods is a science and medical journalist in Washington, D.C. He has won many national writing awards. Mary B. Woods is a school librarian. Their past books include the eight-volume Ancient Technology series. The Woodses have four children. When not writing, reading, or enjoying their grandchildren, they travel to gather material for future books.